1. Count on in 25s from the number in the first box.

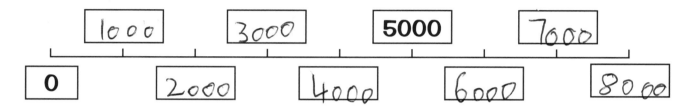

| 0 | 25 | 50 | 75 | 100 | 125 | 150 | 175 | 200 | 225 |

2. Fill in the missing numbers on this number line.

| 1000 | 3000 | **5000** | 7000 |

| **0** | 2000 | 4000 | 6000 | 8000 |

3. Write the numbers these Roman numerals stand for.

a III   3

b VII   7

c L   60

d XLIII   43

e XC   90

f XXXIII   33

g XIX   19

h XXIV   24

4. Complete this number line.

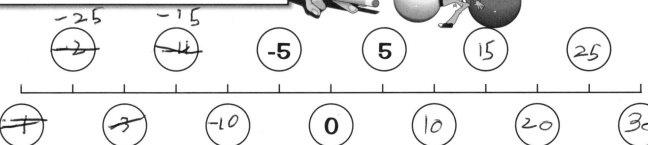

-25   -15   -5   5   15   25

-30   -20   -10   0   10   20   30

Counting and Numbers

1. Count up from zero in...

a ...6s

| 0 | 6 | 12 | 18 | 24 | 30 | 36 | 42 | 48 | 54 |

b ...9s

| 0 | 9 | 18 | 27 | 36 | 45 | 54 | 63 | 72 | 81 |

c ...7s

| 0 | 7 | 14 | 21 | 28 | 35 | 42 | 49 | 56 | 63 |

2. Work out:

a 6 – 8   2

b 2 – 9   7

c 11 – 15   4

d 1 – 8   7

e 16 – 19   3

f 3 – 12   9

3. Write the correct number in each box.

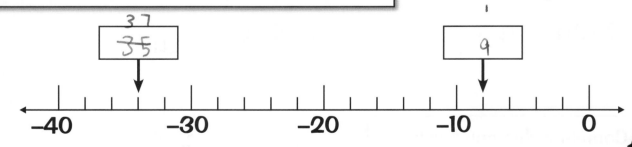

37
35

9

```
-40        -30        -20        -10          0
```

4. The temperature in Fishtown is 13 °C.
What is the new temperature if it falls by:

a 15 °C?   −2   **b** 17 °C?   −4   **c** 20 °C?   −7

Place Value and Ordering

1. Which of these numbers is the biggest? Circle the correct answer.

1764   7164   1764

4671   716   6174

2. Give the value of the underlined digit in each of these numbers.

a 12<u>7</u>4 ....   d 4<u>8</u>59 ....   g 3<u>9</u>41 ....

b <u>6</u>782 ....   e 20<u>3</u>3 ....   h 51<u>6</u>0 ....

c 714<u>6</u> ....   f <u>8</u>258 ....   i 903<u>7</u> ....

3. Use partitioning to complete these sums.

a 5693 = [ ] + 600 + 90 + [ ]

b 2137 = 2000 + [ ] + [ ] + 7

c 7899 = [ ] + [ ] + 90 + [ ]

d 1982 = [ ] + [ ] + [ ] + 2

4. Which of these numbers is the smallest? Circle the correct answer.

9876   987   9981

879   9281   993

Place Value and Ordering

1. Shade in the box showing the smaller amount.

a	3 hundreds	31 tens		d	6 thousands	65 tens
b	9 tens	89 ones		e	8 hundreds	88 tens
c	74 tens	7 hundreds		f	5 tens	55 ones

2. Arrange these numbers in order in the boxes.

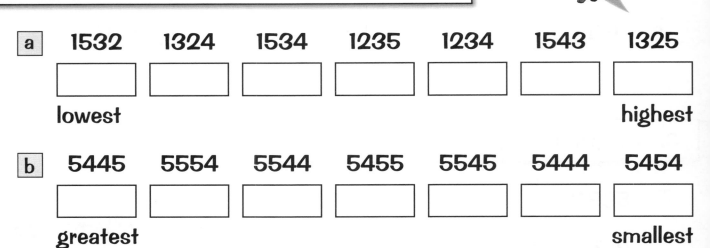

a   1532   1324   1534   1235   1234   1543   1325

lowest   highest

b   5445   5554   5544   5455   5545   5444   5454

greatest   smallest

3. Write down the largest and the smallest number you can make using the digits from the number given.

		largest	smallest				largest	smallest
a	6154				d	8283		
b	1728				e	9341		
c	2967				f	3675		

Place Value and Ordering

1. Write these amounts of money in order starting with the lowest.

a £3990   £3900   £9890   £9808   £9990

lowest   highest

b £8732   £8873   £778   £7789   £7787

lowest   highest

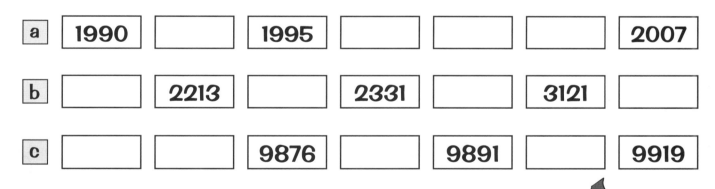

2. Write a number in each empty box so that the numbers are in order from smallest to largest.

a | 1990 | | 1995 | | | | 2007 |

b | | 2213 | | 2331 | | 3121 | |

c | | | 9876 | | 9891 | | 9919 |

3. Write either < or > in each of these boxes.

a 7863 ☐ 7683   **d** 8452 ☐ 8451

b 2456 ☐ 2654   **e** 9989 ☐ 9899

c 5682 ☐ 6852   **f** 2243 ☐ 2324

Adding

---

1. Write the correct number in each box.

1000 more is   1000 more is

a 3614 ⟶ [ ]   **d** [ ] ⟶ 1827

b 1893 ⟶ [ ]   **e** [ ] ⟶ 9899

c 4525 ⟶ [ ]   **f** [ ] ⟶ 8657

---

2. Work out the answers to these column additions.

a
```
    687
 + 129
 ─────
```

b
```
    435
 + 696
 ─────
```

c
```
   3018
 + 3452
 ─────
```

d
```
   5428
 + 4285
 ─────
```

---

3. Write in the missing numbers.

a 1000 cm more than 6342 cm   ....

b 1000 ml more than 8925 ml   ....

c 1000 g more than 9146 g   ....

---

4. Look at these addition squares then fill them in.
The first one has been done for you.

a

420	490	910
370	240	610
790	730	1520

b

	365	650
535		1010
	840	

c

372	186	
	404	699
667		

Adding

---

1. Work out the answers to these sums.

| a | 7 4 8 6
+ 1 6 5 9 | b | 4 6 9 2
+ 2 0 3 3 | c | 3 3 5 9
+ 3 4 7 2 | d | 5 9 7 8
+ 2 4 5 4 |

---

2. Fill in the missing numbers in these charts.

a

+	740	860	590
1470	2210		
3690		4550	
2580			3170

b

+	443	665	809
512			1321
754		1419	
968	1411		

---

3. Write the correct number in each box.

1000 more is

a 10 492 ⟶ ☐

b 15 958 ⟶ ☐

c 82 571 ⟶ ☐

1000 more is

d 98 911 ⟶ ☐

e 39 167 ⟶ ☐

f 9349 ⟶ ☐

---

4. Fill in the missing numbers.

a

```
   3 2 ☐ 2
+  1 ☐ 8 7
 ─────────
  ☐ 6 9 ☐
```

b

```
  ☐ 6 2 ☐
+ 1 3 ☐ 2
 ─────────
  6 ☐ 1 3
```

Adding

1. Work out the answers to these column additions.

a
```
  4 6 0 4
+ 3 3 3 6
─────────
```

b
```
  4 5 7 8
+ 5 3 6 8
─────────
```

c
```
  2 4 5 4
+ 5 9 7 8
─────────
```

d
```
  4 4 6 5
+ 4 9 6 5
─────────
```

e
```
  9 7 6 3
+ 5 6 8 7
─────────
```

f
```
  8 9 2 4
+ 1 4 2 3
─────────
```

2. Solve each problem and write your answers in words.

a Make 1165 greater by 1766.

....

b Find the total of 2378, 2156 and 2439.

....

c Add 1724 to 2347. Then increase your answer by 1000.

....

3. Here's a challenge to your addition skills.

a 112 + 81 + 91 + 3 + 11 = ...

b 8795 + 48 + 233 + 6 = ...

c 950 + 7 + 4289 + 63 = ...

d 9060 + 86 + 786 + 4 = ...

Subtracting

1. Write the correct number in each box.

1000 less is

a	1486	⟶	☐
b	3683	⟶	☐
c	10 891	⟶	☐

1000 less is

d	☐	⟶	972
e	☐	⟶	6934
f	☐	⟶	5701

2. Work out the answers to these column subtractions.

a
```
    7 8 5
 –  4 9 0
 ───────
```

b
```
    6 0 0
 –  5 2 6
 ───────
```

c
```
    8 5 0 6
 –  5 1 9 6
 ─────────
```

d
```
    9 6 4 1
 –  5 1 3 9
 ─────────
```

3. Fill in the missing numbers in these charts.

a

–	583	741	926
65	518		
85		656	
75			851

b

–	2100	3010	4001
1638			2363
1250		1760	
1794	306		

4. Work out the difference between the numbers in each pair.

a	1078 and 651	....
b	4444 and 1234	....
c	9762 and 1936	....

d	7642 and 3248	....
e	2988 and 755	....
f	1816 and 1136	....

Subtracting

---

1. Fill in the missing numbers in these charts.

a

−	4034	7658	9782
2856	1178		
3645		4013	
4021			5761

b

−	8942	7653	9990
5888			4102
6319		1334	
1199	7743		

---

2. Work out the answers to these column subtractions.

a
```
  5 0 0 7
– 4 7 1 1
─────────
```

b
```
  8 7 3 4
– 3 1 7 0
─────────
```

c
```
  7 0 0 0
– 4 7 2 8
─────────
```

d
```
  5 0 7 0
– 4 8 0 1
─────────
```

e
```
  2 8 9 4
– 1 7 9 5
─────────
```

f
```
  9 4 9 1
– 7 2 7 3
─────────
```

g
```
  6 1 1 9
– 5 1 3 7
─────────
```

h
```
  8 0 0 0
– 3 1 0 2
─────────
```

---

3. Write the correct number in each box.

1000 less is

a [   ] ⟶ 8728

b [   ] ⟶ 1304

c [   ] ⟶ 7452

d [   ] ⟶ 5962

1000 less is

e [   ] ⟶ 2508

f [   ] ⟶ 1702

g [   ] ⟶ 74522

h [   ] ⟶ 59621

Subtracting

---

1. Fill in the missing numbers.

a

```
    8 9 □ 4
  -  3 □ 5 □
  ─────────
   □  6 1 2
```

b

```
    4 □ 7 2
  -  □ 9 □ 1
  ─────────
    0 1 2 □
```

---

2. Work out the answers to these column subtractions.

a
```
   8 2 5 9
 - 5 7 8 0
 ─────────
```

b
```
   9 3 5 3
 - 4 3 8 8
 ─────────
```

c
```
   5 3 2 9
 - 5 2 7 8
 ─────────
```

d
```
   2 8 8 3
 - 1 1 9 5
 ─────────
```

---

3. Solve these problems.

a Troy has a jug that holds 2500 ml.
   He puts 1012 ml of water in it. He adds 150 ml of juice.
   How much more liquid can he put in?   ....

b A recipe uses 2700 g of flour.
   Chad has 512 g of flour in one bag and 1224 g in another bag.
   How much more flour does he need?   ....

c Andy ran 1250 m on Monday and 5725 m on Wednesday.
   He wants to run 9000 m this week.
   How much further does he need to run?   ....

Multiplying

1. Work out the missing numbers in these multiplication facts.

a $7 \times 6 =$ ☐   d $9 \times 6 =$ ☐   g $8 \times 6 =$ ☐

b ☐ $\times 9 = 63$ e ☐ $\times 9 = 90$ h ☐ $\times 5 = 45$

c $8 \times$ ☐ $= 64$ f $7 \times$ ☐ $= 35$ i $10 \times$ ☐ $= 80$

2. Complete this multiplication chart.

×	2	6	9	1	4	0	7	3	8	5	10
3			27						24		
5					20		35				
7	14										70

3. Fill in the boxes with 'O' or 'l'.

a $81 \times$ ☐ $= 81$ b $11 \times$ ☐ $= 11$ c $72 \times$ ☐ $= 0$

4. Fill in the missing numbers in these charts.

a

×	50	70	90
3	150		
6		420	
9			810

b

×	80	40	60
8			480
4		160	
12	960		

Multiplying

1. Work out the answers to these multiplication calculations.

| a | 36
× 4 | b | 88
× 9 | c | 73
× 7 | d | 61
× 3 |

| e | 925
× 6 | f | 657
× 7 | g | 243
× 8 | h | 667
× 5 |

2. Write the number in each box that is 5 times larger than the number in the box above it.

| a | 300 | b | 500 | c | 400 | d | 700 |

3. Work out:

a $3 × 4 × 8$ ....

b $9 × 1 × 6$ ....

c $2 × 11 × 5$ ....

d $2 × 6 × 8$ ....

e $5 × 12 × 2$ ....

f $11 × 4 × 3$ ....

4. Circle all the factors of 18 in this list.

| 1 | 3 | 5 | 7 | 9 | 11 | 13 | 15 | 17 |

| 2 | 4 | 6 | 8 | 10 | 12 | 14 | 16 | 18 |

14

Multiplying

---

1. Work out the answers to these multiplication calculations.

a
```
  175
×   7
─────
```

b
```
  495
×   7
─────
```

c
```
  265
×   7
─────
```

d
```
  385
×   7
─────
```

---

2. Draw lines to join these factors of 36 to make factor pairs.

1   2   6   12   9

4   36   3   18   6

---

3. Solve these problems.

a Large boxes of eggs hold 18 eggs. Small boxes hold 6 eggs.
Dean buys 3 large boxes and 2 small boxes of eggs.
How many eggs does he have in total?

....

b Cedric swam 125 lengths on Saturday and 115 lengths on Sunday.
Cho swam four times as far as Cedric.
How many lengths did Cho swim in total?

....

c Pencils cost 67p and pens cost 89p.
Ron bought 4 pencils and 8 pens.
How much did Ron spend?

....

Dviding

1. Work out:

a 88 ÷ 1 ....

b 16 ÷ 4 ....

c 30 ÷ 6 ....

d 64 ÷ 8 ....

e 54 ÷ 9 ....

f 48 ÷ 6 ....

2. Write the correct number in each box.

a 60 —÷ 10→ [ ]

b 5 ——→ [ ]

c 85 ——→ [ ]

d 47 —÷ 100→ [ ]

e 96 ——→ [ ]

f 2 ——→ [ ]

3. Work out the missing numbers in these division facts.

a 81 ÷ 9 = [ ]

b [ ] ÷ 11 = 11

c 63 ÷ [ ] = 7

d 144 ÷ 12 = [ ]

e [ ] ÷ 6 = 4

f 12 ÷ [ ] = 12

g 56 ÷ 8 = [ ]

h [ ] ÷ 10 = 10

i 45 ÷ [ ] = 5

4. Circle the number that is 100 times smaller than 91.

0.91   910   9.1   91.0   0.091   0.901

Dividing

1. Circle the calculation that gives the answer shown.

a

5	45 ÷ 9
	40 ÷ 9

b

3	60 ÷ 12
	36 ÷ 12

c

9	99 ÷ 11
	99 ÷ 9

d

9	54 ÷ 6
	56 ÷ 8

e

11	120 ÷ 12
	132 ÷ 12

f

10	80 ÷ 7
	70 ÷ 7

2. Complete these division charts.

÷	21	35	7	49	70	84	56	28	77	14	42
7	3								11		

÷	63	81	108	27	9	36	99	18	54	45	72
9		9		3							

3. Solve these problems.

a Julia has 72 stamps. She puts 9 on each page of her stamp album.
How many pages will she fill?

....

b Kat has a bag of 50 sweets.
She shares all of the sweets between 5 of her friends.
How many sweets does each friend get?

....

c Cristiano has 108 trophies.
He puts 9 trophies on each shelf of his trophy cabinet.
How many shelves does his cabinet have?

....

Dividing

1. Fill in the missing numbers to make these calculations correct.

a ☐ ÷ 10 = 5.3   **d** 18 ÷ ☐ = 1.8

b 28 ÷ ☐ = 0.28   **e** ☐ ÷ 10 = 190

c ☐ ÷ 100 = 0.08   **f** 77 ÷ ☐ = 0.77

2. Work out these divisions.
   Say how many units, tenths and hundredths each answer has.

a 36 ÷ 10 = ... = ... units .... tenths .... hundredths

b 8 ÷ 100 = ... = ... units .... tenths .... hundredths

c 7 ÷ 10 = ... = ... units .... tenths .... hundredths

3. Solve these problems.

a How many groups of six can be made from fifty four?   ....

b Make four hundred and twenty 10 times smaller.   ....

4. Work out:

a 360 ÷ 60   ....   **d** 960 ÷ 80   ....

b 3500 ÷ 500   ....   **e** 2200 ÷ 200   ....

c 210 ÷ 30   ....   **f** 11 000 ÷ 1000

Estimating

---

1. Round these numbers to the nearest 10.

a 58 .... **b** 63 .... **c** 72 .... **d** 45 ....

---

2. Write your answer to each problem in the first box.
In the second box write the answer to the nearest 100.

a 200 – 70 = [|] **c** 3 × 60 = [|]

b 330 ÷ 3 = [|] **d** 300 + 290 = [|]

---

3. Write a number that is roughly one quarter of the number shown.

a 401 ....   **d** 242 ....   **g** 277 ....

b 119 ....   **e** 219 ....   **h** 321 ....

c 163 ....   **f** 358 ....

---

4. Round each of these numbers to the nearest 10, 100 and 1000.

		nearest 10	nearest 100	nearest 1000
a	3681			
b	7327			
c	5495			
d	9713			

Estimating

1. Circle the best estimate for each of the measurements below.

   a   The length of a pencil   2 mm   20 m   20 cm

   b   The weight of a dog   30 g   30 kg   3 g

2. Round these numbers to the nearest 1000.

   a 7250 ....   c 4500 ....

   b 6100 ....   d 9499 ....

3. Estimate...

   a 128 + 152 = ...   c 122 – 68 = ...

   b 25 ÷ 6 = ...   d 217 – 49 = ...

4. For each of the questions below, write a new calculation that uses the same numbers.

   a 76 × 12 = 912   ☐ ÷ ☐ = ☐

   b 106 + 987 = 1093   ☐ – ☐ = ☐

   c 2497 – 258 = 2239   ☐ + ☐ = ☐

   d 7697 ÷ 179 = 43   ☐ × ☐ = ☐

Fractions and Decimals

---

1. Round these decimal amounts to the nearest whole number.

a **810.4** ....

c **497.9** ....

b **26.5** ....

d **63.2** ....

---

2. Arrange these decimal amounts in order of size.

18.48	14.08	14.84	18.84	14.80	14.48	18.04	18.40

Lowest   Highest

---

3. Do each question the same way as the one done for you.

a $26.47 = \underline{20 + 6 + \frac{4}{10} + \frac{7}{100}}$

d $258.09 = $ ....

b $83.15 = $ ....

e $4.58 = $ ....

c $104.2 = $ ....

f $90.75 = $ ....

---

4. Arrange these amounts in order of size starting with the smallest.

0.5	$\frac{9}{10}$	$\frac{2}{10}$	0.7	$\frac{1}{4}$	$\frac{8}{10}$	0.75	$\frac{1}{10}$

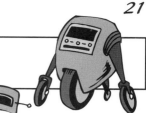

Fractions and Decimals

1. Write the decimal amount that is the same as...

a $\frac{1}{4}$ ....

b $5\frac{3}{10}$ ....

c $\frac{1}{100}$ ....

d $11\frac{4}{10}$ ....

e $2\frac{1}{2}$ ....

f $6\frac{7}{10}$ ....

g $3\frac{5}{10}$ ....

h $\frac{2}{10}$ ....

i $7\frac{1}{10}$ ....

j $8\frac{4}{100}$ ....

k $4\frac{3}{4}$ ....

l $12\frac{9}{10}$ ....

2. Use < or > to show which of each pair is larger.

a 0.76 .... 0.74

b 0.09 .... 0.11

c 0.82 .... 0.91

d $\frac{1}{4}$ 0.23

e 0.12 .... 0.09

f 0.77 .... $\frac{3}{4}$

3. Shade the fraction shown of each shape.

a $\frac{1}{3}$

d $\frac{3}{4}$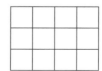

b $\frac{1}{5}$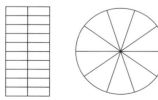

e $\frac{4}{10}$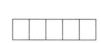

c $\frac{1}{2}$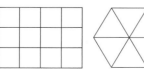

f $\frac{6}{9}$

Fractions and Decimals

1. These number lines count up in $\frac{1}{100}$s. Fill in the missing numbers.

a

$7\frac{46}{100}$					$7\frac{52}{100}$		

b

			$\frac{4}{100}$			$\frac{7}{100}$	

c

	$3\frac{17}{100}$	$3\frac{19}{100}$					

d

			2.97				

e

			$6\frac{31}{100}$				

f

			1.01				

2. Circle the fractions in each question that are equivalent.

a $\frac{2}{8}$ $\frac{3}{7}$ $\frac{1}{4}$ $\frac{3}{6}$ **d** $\frac{9}{10}$ $\frac{2}{7}$ $\frac{1}{4}$ $\frac{3}{12}$

b $\frac{6}{10}$ $\frac{2}{3}$ $\frac{7}{9}$ $\frac{3}{5}$ **e** $\frac{8}{10}$ $\frac{1}{8}$ $\frac{4}{5}$ $\frac{3}{4}$

c $\frac{1}{4}$ $\frac{1}{3}$ $\frac{2}{6}$ $\frac{3}{9}$ **f** $\frac{4}{24}$ $\frac{2}{12}$ $\frac{1}{6}$ $\frac{1}{4}$

3. Circle the number that is $\frac{1}{100}$ of the number on the left.

a 100   0.1   1 $\frac{1}{10}$

b 10   0.01   1 $\frac{1}{10}$

c 1   0.1 $\frac{1}{100}$ $\frac{1}{10}$

Fraction Calculations

---

1. Work out the answers to these fraction calculations.

a $\frac{5}{8} - \frac{4}{8}$ ....

d $\frac{9}{12} - \frac{2}{12}$ ....

b $\frac{11}{42} + \frac{16}{42}$ ....

e $\frac{12}{17} + \frac{1}{17}$ ....

c $\frac{2}{6} + \frac{3}{6}$ ....

f $\frac{19}{23} - \frac{16}{23}$ ....

---

2. Complete these fraction calculations.

a $\frac{5}{8}$ of 48 ....

e $\frac{5}{7}$ of 49 ....

b $\frac{1}{2}$ of 100 ....

f $\frac{2}{3}$ of 33 ....

c $\frac{2}{6}$ of 54 ....

g $\frac{3}{4}$ of 400 ....

d $\frac{3}{5}$ of 60 ....

h $\frac{3}{8}$ of 88 ....

---

3. Work out the answers to these word problems.

a Claire has 48 pairs of shoes. $\frac{3}{4}$ of them are red. How many red pairs of shoes does Claire have? ....

b Lisa has 120 sweets. She gives $\frac{5}{12}$ of them to her brother. How many sweets does Lisa have left? ....

c Cookies come in packets of 12. Chris eats $4\frac{2}{3}$ packets of cookies in one day. How many cookies does he eat? ....

Fraction Calculations

1. Work out the answers to these fraction calculations.

a $\frac{3}{4}$ of 80 + $\frac{1}{2}$ of 8 = ...

c $\frac{3}{8}$ of 16 + $\frac{2}{3}$ of 12 = ...

b $\frac{2}{5}$ of 15 + $\frac{1}{12}$ of 144 = ...

d $\frac{1}{3}$ of 33 + $\frac{5}{9}$ of 27 = ...

2. Fill in the missing fractions in the calculations below.

a .... + $\frac{4}{10}$ = $\frac{9}{10}$

c .... − $\frac{8}{12}$ = $\frac{9}{12}$

b $\frac{4}{17}$ + ... = $\frac{15}{17}$

d $\frac{7}{18}$ + ... = $\frac{15}{18}$

3. Fill in these tables.

a

	$\frac{1}{2}$	$\frac{1}{4}$	$\frac{3}{4}$	$\frac{3}{8}$
of 16				
of 48				
of 8				
of 320				

b

	$\frac{1}{6}$	$\frac{1}{3}$	$\frac{2}{3}$	$\frac{5}{12}$
of 24				
of 36				
of 12				
of 60				

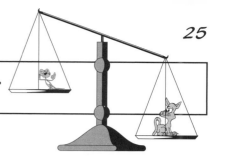

Measuring Problems

---

1.   How many grams are in these masses?

a 1 kg ....

b 5.5 kg ....

c 6.75 kg ....

d 7.25 kg ....

e 2.7 kg ....

f 8.3 kg ....

g 3.25 kg ....

h 9.04 kg ....

---

2.   Solve these problems.

a How many millimetres in 2.4 metres? ....

b Donald's pace measures 70 cm.
How many of his paces measure 7 m? ....

c Seven pieces of string each measure 9 cm.
Find their total length in millimetres. ....

d How much greater is the distance round a rectangle
measuring 8 cm by 36 cm than the distance round
a rectangle measuring 29 cm by 5 cm? ....

---

3.   How many metres are in these distances?

a 7 km ....

b 2.5 km ....

c 4.75 km ....

d 2.29 km ....

Measuring Problems

---

1. Add these centimetre amounts and write your answer in metres.

a	67, 45, 88	e	61, 38, 26 ....
b	38, 53, 59	f	32, 95, 98 ....
c	19, 33, 48	g	47, 65, 48 ....
d	12, 74, 89	h	31, 99, 40 ....

---

2. Calculate the perimeters of these shapes.

a
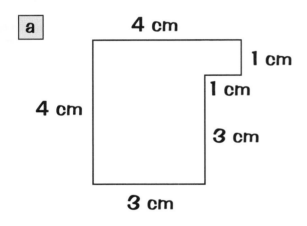

b
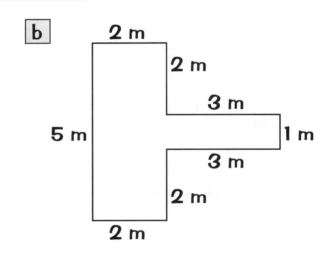

....

---

3. How many minutes are in these times?

a	1 hour 58 minutes	d	4 hours 47 minutes ....
b	2 hours 46 minutes	e	5 hours 12 minutes ....
c	3 hours 45 minutes	f	6 hours 9 minutes ....

Measuring Problems

---

1. **Work out the areas of these shapes.**   Each square is 1 cm²

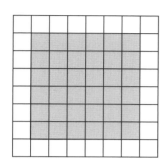   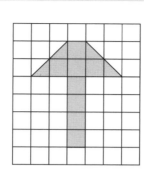   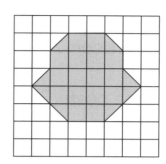   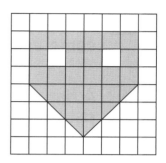

....

---

2. **Add these masses together. Write your answers as mixed numbers.**

a $1\frac{1}{4}$ kg + 4 kg   ....

b $\frac{1}{2}$ kg + 2 kg   ....

c $1\frac{1}{3}$ kg + $3\frac{1}{3}$ kg   ....

d $10\frac{1}{4}$ kg + 12 kg   ....

e $14\frac{1}{12}$ kg + 14 kg   ....

f $8\frac{1}{3}$ kg + $8\frac{1}{3}$ kg   ....

---

3. **Solve these problems.**

a A jar contains 0.46 kg of jam. 175 g of the
jam are used. How many grams of jam are left?   ....

b A pair of scales has 644 g in pan **A** and 296 g in pan **B**.
How many grams must be added to pan **B**
to make the scales balance?   ....

c How many grams must be added to
340 grams to make 1.75 kilograms?   ....

Money Problems

1. Solve these problems.

a How many 5p pieces have the same value as a £1 coin? ....

b A bar of chocolate costs 24p.
Find the cost of four bars. ....

c Share £1.20 equally among three girls.
How many pence does each girl receive? ....

2. Solve these problems. Write the answers in words.

a By how much is 29p more than 14p? ....

b Work out half of £30 and
add £4.00 to your answer. ....

3. Work out the answers to these questions.

a $\frac{1}{4}$ of Bill's money is 18p. Find $\frac{3}{4}$ of his money. ....

b What is the cost of five raffle tickets
priced at 55p each? ....

4. How much change do you get from £5 if you spend...

a £2.37? .... **c** £0.83? .... **e** £1.91? ....

b £3.85? .... **d** £4.62? .... **f** £4.54? ....

Money Problems

1. What is the cost of the following items?

a 3 jigsaws at £4.46 each. ....

b 5 books at £1.30 each. ....

c 7 erasers at 24p each. ....

d 2 toys at £7.75 each. ....

e 4 CDs at £5.99 each. ....

f 6 snacks at 90p each. ....

2. Cross out the calculations that are incorrect.

£1.47 + 76p = £2.23   £1.44 ÷ 6 = 25p   £8.30 – 42p = £7.88

94p + £1.69 = £2.53   93p × 4 = 372p   £3.40 – 54p = £2.84

3. Double each of the amounts below.

a £2.06 ....   **e** £8.58 ....   **i** £5.68 ....

b £7.42 ....   **f** £3.48 ....   **j** £5.34 ....

c £1.52 ....   **g** £6.60 ....   **k** £9.72 ....

d £4.24 ....   **h** £3.18 ....   **l** £7.94 ....

Time Problems

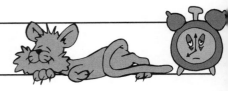

1. **Fill in the gaps in this table.**

a	eight o'clock in the morning	08:00 h	8:00 am
b	seventeen minutes past three in the afternoon		
c		12:00 h	
d	thirteen minutes to four in the morning		
e		00:00 h	

2. **Draw the times in question 1 on these clock faces.**

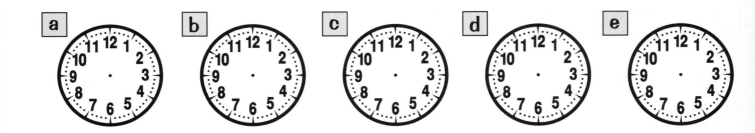

3. **Do these word problems.**

a Sophie spent 36 minutes each day, Monday to Friday, on her homework. How many hours is this in total? ....

b Dominic is 36 months older than his brother who is 13 years old. What age is Dominic? ....

c How many months in thirteen years? ....

d It took John 3 minutes 14 seconds to run a race. How long is this in seconds? ....

Time Problems

1. Write these times as they would appear on a 24-hour clock.

a

pm

....

b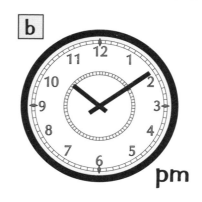

pm

....

c

am

....

2. How many hours are in...

a 3 days 6 hours? ....

c 6 days 19 hours? ....

b 5 days 13 hours? ....

d 2 days 5 hours? ....

3. Write these times as they would appear on a 12-hour clock. Use am or pm.

a 12:17 ....

d 23:44 ....

b 17:20 ....

e 13:35 ....

c 22:00 ....

f 07:05 ....

4. How many days are in...

a 2 weeks 1 day? ....

c 7 weeks 2 days? ....

b 4 weeks 6 days? ....

d 5 weeks 5 days? ....

Shape, Symmetry and Movement

---

1. Name six different 2D shapes.
Write the name and the number of sides for each shape.

1. .... Sides: ....   4. .... Sides: ....

2. .... Sides: ....   5. .... Sides: ....

3. .... Sides: ....   6. .... Sides: ....

---

2. Complete each of these sentences. Choose from the endings given.

a An isosceles triangle...

....

b A scalene triangle...

....

c An equilateral triangle...

....

...is a triangle whose sides are all of different lengths.
...is a triangle with two sides of equal length.
...is a triangle with all three sides the same length.

---

3. Put a tick below the angles that are acute
and a cross below the angles that are obtuse.

Shape, Symmetry and Movement

1. Give the correct name for the 2D shape described by each of these clues.

octagon   rectangle   heptagon   hexagon

triangle   pentagon   circle   polygon

a 6 sides ....

b 8 sides ....

c 5 sides ....

d 3 sides ....

e 7 sides ....

f round ....

g 4 sides, 4 right angles ....

h any shape with straight sides ....

2. Sketch the reflection of each of these shapes.

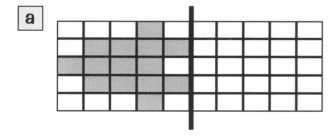

a

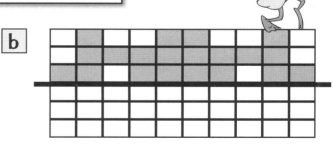

b

3. Colour in the shapes that have at least two lines of symmetry.

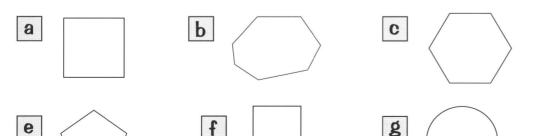

a   **b**   **c**   **d**

e

f

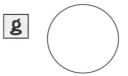

g

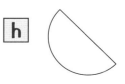

h

Shape, Symmetry and Movement

1. The points at the side of each grid are the coordinates
of the vertices of a shape. Mark the points on the
grid with a cross (x) and name the shape.

a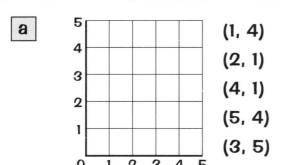

(1, 4)
(2, 1)
(4, 1)
(5, 4)
(3, 5)

....

b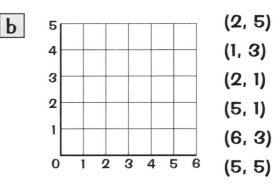

(2, 5)
(1, 3)
(2, 1)
(5, 1)
(6, 3)
(5, 5)

....

c Three of the vertices of a square are (1, 1), (1, 5) and (5, 5).
What are the coordinates of the fourth vertex?

....

2. Complete each of these sentences. Choose from the endings given.

a An acute angle is...

....

b An obtuse angle is...

....

c A protractor is...

....

d A set square is...

....

...a semi-circular instrument for measuring angles.
...an angle more than 90° but less than 180°.
...a flat triangular instrument with 1 right angle.
...a sharply pointed angle whose size is between 0° and 90°.

Shape, Symmetry and Movement

1. Write down the coordinates for each item shown on the grid in the box next to its name.

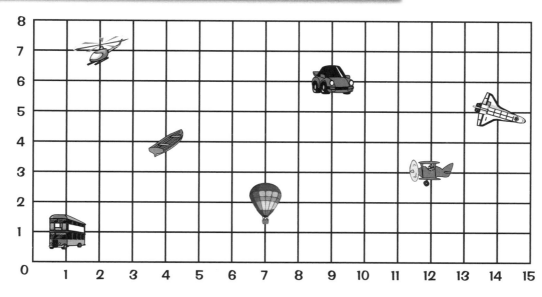

a	helicopter	....
b	air balloon	....
c	aeroplane	....
d	bus	....

e	rocket	....
f	car	....
g	boat	....

2. Describe how you would translate the items on the grid in question 2 in the following ways.

a move the bus to (7, 3)   right 6, up 2
....

b move the car to (5, 1)
....

c move the boat to (14, 2)
....

d move the rocket to (8, 1)
....

Shape, Symmetry and Movement

---

1. Number these angles from 1 to 6, with 1 being the smallest angle.

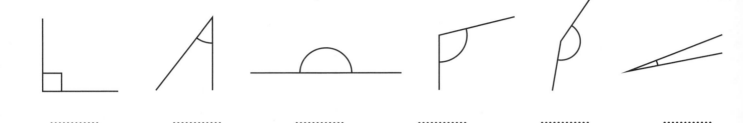

....

---

2. Explain the difference between an isosceles triangle and an equilateral triangle.

....

....

---

3. Use a ruler to draw reflections of these shapes.

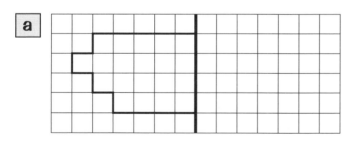

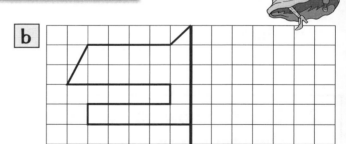

---

4. What will the new coordinates of point A be after these translations?

a Left 3, up 4 ....

b Right 2, up 1 ....

c Right 4, down 4 ....

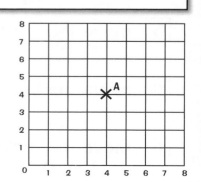

Using Data

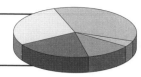

1. Below is a graph of Robert's journey from home to the leisure centre. Use it to answer these questions.

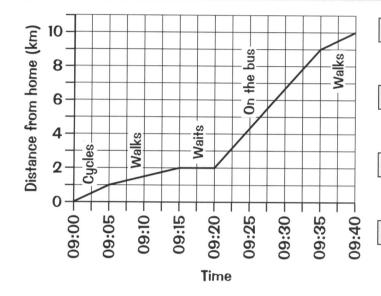

a What time does Robert leave home? ....

b How far does he cycle? ....

c How long does he wait for the bus? ....

d How long does the whole journey take? ....

2. This table shows the number of ice creams sold by an ice cream van over four days. Use it to help you answer these questions.

Ice Cream Flavour	Number Sold				TOTALS
	Thurs	Fri	Sat	Sun	
Vanilla	14	19	41	49	
Chocolate	25	31	40	44	
Strawberry	17	15	17	20	
Bubblegum	8	0	14	20	
Mint Choc Chip	12	23	19	36	
TOTALS					

a Fill in the Totals column and row in the table above.

b Which flavour sold the most over the four days? ....

c On which day was the most ice cream sold? ....

d How many more ice creams were sold on Saturday than Thursday? ....

Using Data

> **1.** Use the bar chart to answer these questions.

a What is the maximum temperature in:

February? ....

April? ....

October? ....

August? ....

June? ....

March? ....

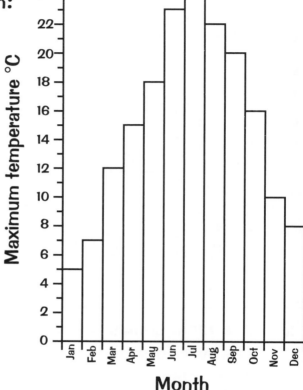

b Which month has the hottest maximum temperature? ....

c Which month has a maximum temperature of 5 °C? ....

d How many months have a maximum temperature greater than 9 °C? ....

e What is the difference between the maximum temperatures in March and September? ....

f Which month has a maximum temperature warmer than February but colder than November? ....

Using Data

1. A group of children chose their favourite colours. The results are shown in the table. Complete the unfinished bar chart to show the results given in the table. Then answer the questions below.

Colour	Children
red	40
blue	25
green	10
yellow	30
orange	35

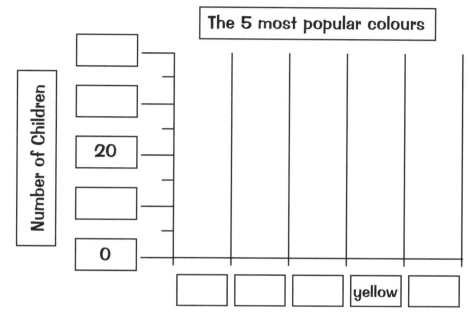

The 5 most popular colours

Number of Children

20

0

yellow

a Which two colours together had the same number of votes as orange? ....

b Which was the most popular colour? ....

c How many more people preferred orange to blue? ....

d How many people in total liked the two most popular colours? ....

e How many children altogether liked the two least popular colours? ....

f Which colour was three times as popular as green? ....

g Which colour received only a quarter as many votes as red? ....

h How many children were involved in doing the survey? ....

40

Using Data

1. Below is a pictogram to show the number of goals scored by different players on a football team, over one season.
Use the information in the pictogram below to answer the questions.

 = 4 goals   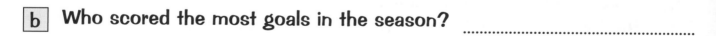 = 2 goals

Player	Goals scored	Total
Rio Strike	⚽ ⚽ ⚽ ⚽ ◖	
Oscar Side		9
Mark Dribble		7
Keith Kicker		18
Owen Goal	⚽ ⚽ ◖	
Ned Field	⚽ ⚽ ◕	

a Fill in the gaps in the pictogram above.

b Who scored the most goals in the season? ....

c How many more goals did Keith Kicker score than Ned Field? ....

d Who scored half as many goals as Keith Kicker? ....

e How many goals behind the highest scorer was Owen Goal? ....

Answers — Pages 1 to 12

PAGE 1
Q1. (0), 25, 50, 75, 100, 125, 150, 175, 200, 225
Q2. (0), 1000, 2000, 3000, 4000, (5000), 6000, 7000, 8000
Q3. a) 3   b) 7
    c) 50   d) 43
    e) 90   f) 33
    g) 19   h) 24
Q4. -30, -25, -20, -15, -10, (-5), (0), (5), 10, 15, 20, 25, 30

PAGE 2
Q1. a) (0), 6, 12, 18, 24, 30, 36, 42, 48, 54
    b) (0), 9, 18, 27, 36, 45, 54, 63, 72, 81
    c) (0), 7, 14, 21, 28, 35, 42, 49, 56, 63
Q2. a) -2   b) -7
    c) -4   d) -7
    e) -3   f) -9
Q3. -34, -8
Q4. a) -2 °C   b) -4 °C
    c) -7 °C

PAGE 3
Q1. 7164
Q2. a) 70   b) 6000
    c) 6   d) 800
    e) 30   f) 8000
    g) 900   h) 60
    i) 7
Q3. a) 5000, 3
    b) 100, 30
    c) 7000, 800, 9
    d) 1000, 900, 80
Q4. 879

PAGE 4
Q1. a) 3 hundreds
    b) 89 ones
    c) 7 hundreds
    d) 65 tens
    e) 8 hundreds
    f) 5 tens
Q2. a) 1234, 1235, 1324, 1325, 1532, 1534, 1543
    b) 5554, 5545, 5544, 5455, 5454, 5445, 5444
Q3. a) 6541, 1456
    b) 8721, 1278
    c) 9762, 2679
    d) 8832, 2388
    e) 9431, 1349
    f) 7653, 3567

PAGE 5
Q1. a) £3900, £3990, £9808, £9890, £9990
    b) £778, £7787, £7789, £8732, £8873
Q2. a), b) and c)
    Any suitable numbers so that numbers are in increasing order.
Q3. a) >   b) <
    c) <   d) >
    e) >   f) <

PAGE 6
Q1. a) 4614   b) 2893
    c) 5525   d) 827
    e) 8899   f) 7657
Q2. a) 816   b) 1131
    c) 6470   d) 9713
Q3. a) 7342 cm   b) 9925 ml
    c) 10 146 g
Q4. a) completed example
    b) 285, (365), (650) (535), 475, (1010) 820, (840), 1660
    c) (372), (186), 558 295, (404), (699) (667), 590, 1257

PAGE 7
Q1. a) 9145   b) 6725
    c) 6831   d) 8432
Q2. a) (2210), 2330, 2060 4430, (4550), 4280 3320, 3440, (3170)
    b) 955, 1177, (1321) 1197, (1419), 1563 (1411), 1633, 1777
Q3. a) 11 492   b) 16 958
    c) 83 571   d) 99 911
    e) 40 167   f) 10 349
Q4. a) (3) (2) 1 (2) (1) 4 (8) (7) 4 (6) (9) 9
    b) 4 (6) (2) 1 (1) (3) 9 (2) (6) 0 (1) (3)

PAGE 8
Q1. a) 7940   b) 9946
    c) 8432   d) 9430
    e) 15 450   f) 10 347
Q2. a) two thousand, nine hundred and thirty one
    b) six thousand, nine hundred and seventy three
    c) five thousand and seventy one
Q3. a) 298   b) 9082
    c) 5309   d) 9936

PAGE 9
Q1. a) 486   b) 2683
    c) 9891   d) 1972
    e) 7934   f) 6701
Q2. a) 295   b) 74
    c) 3310   d) 4502
Q3. a) (518), 676, 861 498, (656), 841 508, 666, (851)
    b) 462, 1372, (2363) 850, (1760), 2751 (306), 1216, 2207
Q4. a) 427   b) 3210
    c) 7826   d) 4394
    e) 2233   f) 680

PAGE 10
Q1. a) (1178), 4802, 6926 389, (4013), 6137 13, 3637, (5761)
    b) 3054, 1765, (4102) 2623, (1334), 3671 (7743), 6454, 8791
Q2. a) 296   b) 5564
    c) 2272   d) 269
    e) 1099   f) 2218
    g) 982   h) 4898
Q3. a) 9728   b) 2304
    c) 8452   d) 6962
    e) 3508   f) 2702
    g) 75 522   h) 60 621

PAGE 11
Q1. a) (8) (9) 6 (4) (3) 3 (5) 2 5 (6) (1) (2)
    b) (4) 0 (7) (2) 3 (9) 5 (1) (0) (1) (2) 1
Q2. a) 2479   b) 4965
    c) 51   d) 1688
Q3. a) 1338 ml   b) 964 g
    c) 2025 m

PAGE 12
Q1. a) 42   b) 7
    c) 8   d) 54
    e) 10   f) 5
    g) 48   h) 9
    i) 8
Q2. 6, 18, (27), 3, 12, 0, 21, 9, (24), 15, 30
10, 30, 45, 5, (20), 0, (35), 15, 40, 25, 50
(14), 42, 63, 7, 28, 0, 49, 21, 56, 35, (70)
Q3. a) 1   b) 1
    c) 0
Q4. a) (150), 210, 270 300, (420), 540 450, 630, (810)
    b) 640, 320, (480) 320, (160), 240 (960), 480, 720

Answers — Pages 13 to 23

PAGE 13
Q1. a) 144   b) 792
    c) 511   d) 183
    e) 5550   f) 4599
    g) 1944   h) 3335
Q2. a) 1500   b) 2500
    c) 2000   d) 3500
Q3. a) 96   b) 54
    c) 110   d) 96
    e) 120   f) 132
Q4.   1, 2, 3, 6, 9 and 18 should
      be circled.

PAGE 14
Q1. a) 1225   b) 3465
    c) 1855   d) 2695
Q2.   1 — 36, 2 — 18, 6 — 6,
      12 — 3, 4 — 9
Q3. a) 66 eggs b) 960 lengths
    c) 980p/£9.80

PAGE 15
Q1. a) 88   b) 4
    c) 5   d) 8
    e) 6   f) 8
Q2. a) 6   b) 0.5
    c) 8.5   d) 0.47
    e) 0.96   f) 0.02
Q3. a) 9   b) 121
    c) 9   d) 12
    e) 24   f) 1
    g) 7   h) 100
    i) 9
Q4.   0.91

PAGE 16
Q1. a) 45 ÷ 9   b) 36 ÷ 12
    c) 99 ÷ 11 d) 54 ÷ 6
    e) 132 ÷ 12 f) 70 ÷ 7
Q2.   (3), 5, 1, 7, 10, 12, 8, 4, (11), 2,
      6
      7, (9), 12, (3), 1, 4, 11, 2, 6, 5,
      8
Q3. a) 8 pages b) 10 sweets
    c) 12 shelves

PAGE 17
Q1. a) 53   b) 100
    c) 8   d) 10
    e) 1900   f) 100
Q2. a) 3.6 = 3 units, 6 tenths,
       0 hundredths
    b) 0.08 = 0 units, 0 tenths,
       8 hundredths
    c) 0.7 = 0 units, 7 tenths,
       0 hundredths
Q3. a) 9   b) 42
Q4. a) 6   b) 7
    c) 7   d) 12
    e) 11   f) 11

PAGE 18
Q1. a) 60   b) 60
    c) 70   d) 50
Q2. a) 130, 100 b) 110, 100
    c) 180, 200 d) 590, 600
Q3.   Accept any sensible answer,
      for example:
    a) 100   b) 30
    c) 40   d) 60
    e) 55   f) 90
    g) 70   h) 80
Q4. a) 3680, 3700, 4000
    b) 7330, 7300, 7000
    c) 5500, 5500, 5000
    d) 9710, 9700, 10 000

PAGE 19
Q1. a) 20 cm   b) 30 kg
Q2. a) 7000   b) 6000
    c) 5000   d) 9000
Q3.   Your answers should be in the
      following ranges:
    a) 275 to 285
    b) 3 to 5   c) 45 to 55
    d) 165 to 175
Q4. a) 912 ÷ 76 = 12 or
       912 ÷ 12 = 76
    b) 1093 − 987 = 106 or
       1093 − 106 = 987
    c) 2239 + 258 = 2497 or
       258 + 2239 = 2497
    d) 179 × 43 = 7697 or
       43 × 179 = 7697

PAGE 20
Q1. a) 810   b) 27
    c) 498   d) 63
Q2.   14.08, 14.48, 14.80, 14.84,
      18.04, 18.40, 18.48, 18.84
Q3. a) $20 + 6 + \frac{4}{10} + \frac{7}{100}$
    b) $80 + 3 + \frac{1}{10} + \frac{5}{100}$
    c) $100 + 4 + \frac{2}{10}$
    d) $200 + 50 + 8 + \frac{9}{100}$
    e) $4 + \frac{5}{10} + \frac{8}{100}$
    f) $90 + \frac{7}{10} + \frac{5}{100}$
Q4. $\frac{1}{10}$, $\frac{2}{10}$, $\frac{1}{4}$, 0.5, 0.7,
      0.75, $\frac{8}{10}$, $\frac{9}{10}$

PAGE 21
Q1. a) 0.25   b) 5.3
    c) 0.01   d) 11.4
    e) 2.5   f) 6.7
    g) 3.5   h) 0.2
    i) 7.1   j) 8.04
    k) 4.75   l) 12.9
Q2. a) >   b) <
    c) <   d) >
    e) >   f) >
Q3. a) Any 3 boxes shaded.
       Any 4 boxes shaded.
    b) Any 4 boxes shaded.
       Any 2 boxes shaded.
    c) Any 6 boxes shaded.
       Any 3 boxes shaded.
    d) Any 9 boxes shaded.
       Any 6 boxes shaded.
    e) Any 2 boxes shaded.
       Any 8 boxes shaded.
    f) Any 2 boxes shaded.
       Any 8 boxes shaded.

PAGE 22
Q1. a) $(7\frac{46}{100})$, $7\frac{47}{100}$, $7\frac{48}{100}$, $7\frac{49}{100}$, $7\frac{50}{100}$,
       $7\frac{51}{100}$, $(7\frac{52}{100})$, $7\frac{53}{100}$, $7\frac{54}{100}$
    b) 0, $\frac{1}{100}$, $\frac{2}{100}$, $\frac{3}{100}$, $(\frac{4}{100})$, $\frac{5}{100}$, $\frac{6}{100}$,
       $(\frac{7}{100})$, $\frac{8}{100}$
    c) $3\frac{15}{100}$, $3\frac{16}{100}$, $(3\frac{17}{100})$, $3\frac{18}{100}$, $(3\frac{19}{100})$,
       $3\frac{20}{100}$, $3\frac{21}{100}$, $3\frac{22}{100}$, $3\frac{23}{100}$
    d) 2.93, 2.94, 2.95, 2.96, (2.97),
       2.98, 2.99, 3.00, 3.01
    e) $6\frac{27}{100}$, $6\frac{28}{100}$, $6\frac{29}{100}$, $6\frac{30}{100}$, $(6\frac{31}{100})$,
       $6\frac{32}{100}$, $6\frac{33}{100}$, $6\frac{34}{100}$, $6\frac{35}{100}$
    f) 0.97, 0.98, 0.99, 1.00, (1.01),
       1.02, 1.03, 1.04, 1.05
Q2. a) $\frac{2}{8}$, $\frac{1}{4}$ b) $\frac{6}{10}$, $\frac{3}{5}$
    c) $\frac{1}{3}$, $\frac{2}{6}$, $\frac{3}{9}$
    d) $\frac{1}{4}$, $\frac{3}{12}$ e) $\frac{8}{10}$, $\frac{4}{5}$
    f) $\frac{4}{24}$, $\frac{2}{12}$, $\frac{1}{6}$
Q3. a) 1   b) $\frac{1}{10}$
    c) $\frac{1}{100}$

PAGE 23
Q1. a) $\frac{1}{8}$ b) $\frac{27}{42}$
    c) $\frac{5}{6}$ d) $\frac{7}{12}$
    e) $\frac{13}{17}$ f) $\frac{3}{23}$
Q2. a) 30   b) 50
    c) 18   d) 36
    e) 35   f) 22
    g) 300   h) 33
Q3. a) 36   b) 70
    c) 56

Answers — Pages 24 to 34

PAGE 24
Q1. a) 64   b) 18
    c) 14   d) 26
Q2. a) $\frac{5}{10}$ $(= \frac{1}{2})$
    b) $\frac{11}{17}$
    c) $\frac{17}{12}$ $(= 1\frac{5}{12})$
    d) $\frac{8}{18}$ $(= \frac{4}{9})$
Q3. a) 8, 4, 12, 6
      24, 12, 36, 18
      4, 2, 6, 3
      160, 80, 240, 120
    b) 4, 8, 16, 10
      6, 12, 24, 15
      2, 4, 8, 5
      10, 20, 40, 25

PAGE 25
Q1. a) 1000 g   b) 5500 g
    c) 6750 g   d) 7250 g
    e) 2700 g   f) 8300 g
    g) 3250 g   h) 9040 g
Q2. a) 2400 mm
    b) 10   c) 630 mm
    d) 20 cm
Q3. a) 7000 m   b) 2500 m
    c) 4750 m   d) 2290 m

PAGE 26
Q1. a) 2 m   b) 1.5 m
    c) 1 m   d) 1.75 m
    e) 1.25 m   f) 2.25 m
    g) 1.6 m   h) 1.7 m
Q2. a) 16 cm   b) 20 m
Q3. a) 118 minutes
    b) 166 minutes
    c) 225 minutes
    d) 287 minutes
    e) 312 minutes
    f) 369 minutes

PAGE 27
Q1. a) 36 cm²   b) 10 cm²
    c) 20 cm²   d) 25 cm²
Q2. a) $5\frac{1}{4}$ kg   b) $2\frac{1}{2}$ kg
    c) $4\frac{2}{3}$ kg   d) $22\frac{1}{4}$ kg
    e) $28\frac{1}{12}$ kg   f) $16\frac{2}{3}$ kg
Q3. a) 285 g   b) 348 g
    c) 1410 g

PAGE 28
Q1. a) 20   b) 96p
    c) 40p
Q2. a) fifteen pence
    b) nineteen pounds
Q3. a) 54p   b) £2.75/275p
Q4. a) £2.63   b) £1.15
    c) £4.17   d) £0.38/38p
    e) £3.09   f) £0.46/46p

PAGE 29
Q1. a) £13.38   b) £6.50
    c) £1.68   d) £15.50
    e) £23.96   f) £5.40
Q2. These should be crossed out:
    94p + £1.69 = £2.53
    £1.44 ÷ 6 = 25p
    £3.40 – 54p = £2.84
Q3. a) £4.12   b) £14.84
    c) £3.04   d) £8.48
    e) £17.16   f) £6.96
    g) £13.20   h) £6.36
    i) £11.36   j) £10.68
    k) £19.44   l) £15.88

PAGE 30
Q1. a) (eight o'clock in the morning, 08:00 h, 8:00 am)
    b) (seventeen minutes past three in the afternoon), 15:17 h, 3:17 pm
    c) midday/noon/twelve o'clock in the afternoon, (12:00 h) 12:00 pm
    d) (thirteen minutes to four in the morning), 03:47 h, 3:47 am
    e) midnight, twelve o'clock in the morning, (00:00 h), 12:00 am
Q2. a)   b)
    c)   d)
    e)
Q3. a) 3 hours   b) 16 years old
    c) 156 months
    d) 194 seconds

PAGE 31
Q1. a) 15:00   b) 22:09
    c) 01:52
Q2. a) 78 hours   b) 133 hours
    c) 163 hours   d) 53 hours
Q3. a) 12:17 pm   b) 5:20 pm
    c) 10:00 pm   d) 11:44 pm
    e) 1:35 pm   f) 07:05 am
Q4. a) 15 days   b) 34 days
    c) 51 days   d) 40 days

PAGE 32
Q1. Possible answers:
circle 1, semi-circle 2, triangle 3, square 4, rectangle 4, oblong 4, pentagon 5, quadrilateral 4, hexagon 6, heptagon 7, octagon 8.
Q2. a) (An isosceles triangle)… is a triangle with two sides of equal length.
    b) (A scalene triangle)… is a triangle whose sides are all of different lengths.
    c) (An equilateral triangle)… is a triangle with all three sides the same length.
Q3. ✗, ✔, ✗, ✔, ✗, ✔

PAGE 33
Q1. a) hexagon   b) octagon
    c) pentagon   d) triangle
    e) heptagon   f) circle
    g) rectangle   h) polygon
Q2. a)
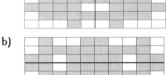
    b)
Q3. The following shapes should be coloured:
a, c, d, e, f, g

PAGE 34
Q1. a)
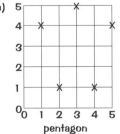
pentagon
    b)
hexagon
    c) (5, 1)

Q2. a) (An acute angle is)... a sharply pointed angle whose size is between 0° and 90°.

　　b) (An obtuse angle is)... an angle more than 90° but less than 180°.

　　c) (A protractor is)... a semi-circular instrument for measuring angles.

　　d) (A set square is)... a flat triangular instrument with 1 right angle.

PAGE 35

Q1. a) 2, 7　　b) 7, 2
　　c) 12, 3　　d) 1, 1
　　e) 14, 5　　f) 9, 6
　　g) 4, 4

Q2. a) (right 6, up 2)
　　b) left 4, down 5
　　c) right 10, down 2
　　d) left 6, down 4

PAGE 36

Q1. 3, 2, 6, 4, 5, 1

Q2. An equilateral triangle has all three sides the same length and all angles equal, but an isosceles triangle has only two sides of equal length and only two equal angles.

Q3. a)

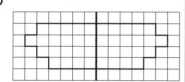

　　b)

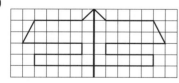

Q4. a) (1, 8)　　b) (6, 5)
　　c) (8, 0)

PAGE 37

Q1. a) 09:00　　b) 1 km
　　c) 5 minutes
　　d) 40 minutes

Q2. a) Rows: 123, 140, 69, 42, 90
　　　　Columns: 76, 88, 131, 169
　　b) Chocolate
　　c) Sunday
　　d) 55

PAGE 38

Q1. a) February: 7 °C
　　　　April: 15 °C
　　　　October: 16 °C
　　　　August: 22 °C
　　　　June: 23 °C
　　　　March: 12 °C
　　b) July　　c) January
　　d) 9　　e) 8 °C
　　f) December

PAGE 39

Q1.

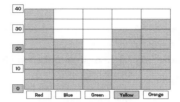

　　a) blue and green
　　b) red　　c) 10
　　d) 75　　e) 35
　　f) yellow　　g) green
　　h) 140

PAGE 40

Q1. a)

Player	Goals scored	Total
Rio Strike	⚽⚽⚽⚽⚽	17
Oscar Side	⚽⚽⚽	9
Mark Dribble	⚽⚽	7
Keith Kicker	⚽⚽⚽⚽⚽	18
Owen Goal	⚽⚽⚽	10
Ned Field	⚽⚽⚽	11

　　b) Keith Kicker
　　c) 7　　d) Oscar Side
　　e) 8